Pragmatic Wisdom Vol. 1

Stoic Lessons on Work and Retirement

James Bellerjeau

A Fine Idea

Contents

Chapter One

Why Do Anything?

An Introduction to the Stoic Lessons

D ear friends. Join me on a journey to discover what it means to live a good life. Our inspiration in this quest is Seneca's Moral Letters to Lucilius, revisited and revised for our modern times. The search for what it means to live a good life was not new in Seneca's day, and it will not be old when we are all long gone.

Although these are not Seneca's letters, they honor both his wisdom and his instructions for new students. That is, we should grapple with deep thoughts and make our understanding of the truth personal.

Because no one has a monopoly on the truth, we can each contribute to the puzzle. **The reason to do anything is to answer a question that has not been answered, or at a minimum to answer it for yourself.**

In answering life's deepest questions, would it not be foolish for us to pass by the foundational stones laid by the great thinkers who labored before us? Seneca himself in search of inspiration says in his Letter 2:

> I am wont to cross over even into the enemy's
> camp, — not as a deserter, but as a scout.

Let us all be avid scouts of the great thinkers, seeking out their every camp with the mindset of anthropologists unearthing meaning from among the ruins. Although Seneca's words have been mined by many for centuries, each generation keeps turning up gemstones.

Thus, with this series of Pragmatic Wisdom for Busy People, let us polish old stones to show them in a new light, and in washing off the mud and debris, reveal what fresh reflections may appear.

Be well.

PS — You can read each of the volumes independently, as it suits your time and your interests. Dedicated readers will find, however, that their understanding of each volume will increase upon reading further volumes. The sincere student may therefore wish to have the full set of Stoic letters: Pragmatic Wisdom for the Sincere Student.

Chapter Two

On Being Busy

Better an hour spent in quiet contemplation than a year mindlessly doing

G reetings dear reader!

Do not call yourself busy. Busyness is the fate of those who have relinquished control over their daily lives. They have ceded ground not honorably, like the battered general calling retreat to the troops after a hard-fought battle.

No, the busy today have put their fortune in the hands of strangers. They have done so without a fight and often without a thought. If you do not maintain the strictest control over your calendar, like a miser clutching his last coin, you will find your ledger soon overflowing, but with obligations, not credits.

Fear of missing out you say? Tell me, when did a mindless herd of cattle ever lead you to a destination you wanted to go to? You not only exhaust yourself trying to keep up with the herd, but you also end up bedraggled, dusty, and dung-riddled for your efforts. And no sooner has the lead cow paused than a random bull becomes the leader of the next charge.

Fear of becoming irrelevant you say? Show me a person who does not fear they are missing out, and I will show you a person who understands precisely the value of their time. I would rather hear a single person who says "No" calmly, than a hundred who vigorously cry out "Yes!"

Time that you do not waste is a deposit in the bank account of your life. The sheep stuff their day with the filling but ultimately empty blandishments of modern media. The more generously you cut out their bleating, the more you will clear your schedule, not to mention your head.

It's the busy person who occupies themselves with doing. But doing without thinking is the fate of beasts of burden, not you. With apologies to the Goddess of Victory, don't just do it!

Better an hour spent in quiet contemplation than a year mindlessly doing.

Be well.

Chapter Three

On the Teacher's Duty

Just because I am alone does not mean I am wasting my hours away

"**D**o you advise me," you ask, "to ghost the public sphere, and to be happy with my thoughts alone? How am I helping improve the world by withdrawing from society?"

This is not the contradiction that first appears. My aim in seeking seclusion is to create space for great work. Just because I am alone does not mean I am wasting my hours away. I hope that by taking time to think clearly, I can add to the storehouse of ideas as a service to all who come after me.

For all those who cannot see where they are walking because their faces are planted in their iPhones, it is my life's labor to remove stones from the path, so that we do not needlessly stumble.

Here is what I would tell them: Don't worry about what others think. Decide for yourself what success and happiness mean.

Rather than rejoicing in your latest raise, ask whether you are painting your silver handcuffs now with gold. Do you call your gilded shackles progress? If you wish to live happily, your every thought must be to disdain the normal trappings of success that hold so many in their spell.

We think possessions will satisfy us when all they really do is whet our appetites for more. The most unfulfilling meal is the lavish one you have given your very life to obtain. And worse, maintaining your standard of living at the highest-level chains you to a treadmill whose controls only ratchet upwards.

This shall be your rule of thumb — strive for functionality over form.

- Your feet and a bicycle will get you to most places as quickly or better than a Rolls Royce, and they're easier to park.

- A picnic lunch of a cheese sandwich by the lake will satisfy you as much or more than a feast of *foie gras* and lobster.

- Your Patek Philippe grand complication chronograph tells time not a whit better than a Timex automatic.

Adapt your circumstances to succeed with simple things, and you will train your mind in sufficiency.

I hear you asking "How do I reconcile a life of contemplation with the need to pay my bills?" Just as the opposite of busyness is not idleness, so too when you give up wants you do not become free of needs.

It is noble to work according to your nature and abilities to sustain yourself. The satisfaction of a job well done is its own reward, besides keeping your ledger in the black, and is also one of the paths to finding meaning.

When I tease out such lessons for myself and future generations, am I not providing a greater service than when I review the hundredth sales contract, draft the latest annual report, or rage on in Twitter wars?

Rather trust that at least some who are seen least in the public eye are engaged in higher pursuits.

But now I stop and balance the scales with a contribution in kind. I pay not with my own currency, but with that of the Chinese philosopher Confucius:

> The more man meditates upon good thoughts,
> the better will be his world and the world at large.

I expect you are wondering why I am quoting other philosophers to such an extent, rather than relying on the established Stoic canon. Can the Stoics lay claim to being the only ones to have laid bare and mined a rich vein of wisdom?

If the Greeks and Romans themselves never pretended to have had every worthy thought, then why should we?

Nothing brings me greater joy than to know that great thoughts have emerged and re-emerged from every corner of the globe, across time and distance. I trawl willingly the waters of Asia, Europe, and the Americas, and my travels have not gone unrewarded.

You, my sincere student, may take this as a free gift, for it is not mine to hoard but the world's to share.

From the Japanese Zen, my nets have hauled up this treasure, reminding us that it is not only the teacher who has a duty:

> To a sincere student, every day is a fortunate day.
> Time passes but he never lags behind. Neither
> glory nor shame can move him.

Be well.

Chapter Four

On Retirement

How much better to choose the time of your leaving yourself?

I am never so happy as when my mailbox yields an e-mail from you. They contain confirmation of your progress, and this is no small thing. I urge you to continue on in this way, and this urging is for your benefit more than any other.

You are now at the point where you must decide the next stage of your life: Will you stay on the raging white waters, bending your oar to keep the ship straight, or will you turn off onto a quieter tributary, where eventually all the waters will end up?

You face the deliberate choice of whether to slow your pace, ease your burden, and let someone else serve as captain.

Though some swear they will die tethered to the helm, and will even go down with the ship, it is only natural to pack it all in when the load that once seemed light starts to weigh you down.

How much better to choose the time of your leaving yourself? You otherwise risk others choosing it for you in circumstances that are unlikely to be to your liking.

"I am still at the peak of my powers," you say. "What if I am leaving too early?" So, no one is yet pushing you out the door. What is it exactly that has you clinging to your desk?

Ambition is what got you to your current position. Will you let ambition goad you on for the sake of accomplishment alone?

You need no further accolades to know you have achieved more than most. Your competitive nature is what gave you the drive to succeed, but will you let it drive you into an early grave?

Even the fastest racehorse will lose the race of time, and in the waning years will lose to many lesser horses she could have bested in her prime. Why stay on the field when the odds are inevitably stacked against you?

There is a certain pride some people take in knowing they have accumulated more wealth and possessions than their peers. I have warned you many times about the dangers of measuring your worth by your holdings.

If you need reinforcement beyond my own words, I can give it to you from an authoritative voice in the form of Seneca himself:

> No one is compelled to pursue prosperity at top
> speed; it means something to call a halt … instead
> of pressing eagerly after favoring fortune.

Seneca understood that the choices we make voluntarily are the most meaningful compared to the ones that are forced upon us.

A well-ordered mind can find peace with either, but the choices you make when no one is making you are the ones that make you who you are.

Any voluntary choice carries risks, but what of it? Firstly, nothing of value is gained without effort and risk. Did you gain your current position without taking any chances? Looking back over your life so far, were there not many skirmishes where you emerged the victor but could have been vanquished?

And secondly, remember that you are always choosing, whether you do it by design or by default: if you choose not to decide, you still have made a choice. (Lest you think I borrow too freely without settling my accounts, I give thanks for this formulation of wisdom to the Canadian band Rush in their song Freewill.)

So age and decrepitude will have their way with you, whether you prepare for their workings or hold your breath and hope to wish them away. And that's if you are lucky, for a long life is not guaranteed to any of us.

You have long since passed the point of having what you need. Have you reached the point of having enough?

Every luxury you learn to live without is a payment on the insurance policy for a happy life. Fine food, expensive wine, sports cars, vacation homes; you can have them all and enjoy them all, but they will all be taken from you, one by one, as surely as the grains of sand drop from the top of the hourglass to the bottom. He that fortifies himself by relinquishing such pleasures voluntarily will suffer no loss from their absence.

My sayings above may have settled our accounts to today, but I wish to be sure I am not leaving you expecting more. I thus draw once more from the reserves of Seneca, who says:

> If you keep turning round and looking about,
> in order to see how much you may carry away

with you, and how much money you may keep
to equip yourself for the life of leisure, you will
never find a way out. No man can swim ashore
and take his baggage with him.

It is in anticipation of luxury and the accumulation of things
that we forget the best things cannot be acquired with money.
The best-rewarded effort is the work we put into ourselves.

Be well.

Chapter Five

On Posterity

We want some part of us to continue, to survive the ages

"How will I be remembered?" Is this what is keeping you from letting go of your position, dear reader?

I ask you, are you making a mark only insofar and for so long as you are holding the reins of power? There is no end to powerful people who are forgotten the moment they step foot out their office doors.

But you would be mistaken in thinking that it is your office that makes you memorable.

Let's consider what makes someone noteworthy not just in the moment, but for posterity.

- We can all bring to mind great literature and art, and often, though not always, this is intimately tied to the name of its creator.

- Renown declines rapidly when we consider music, where there is but a handful of composers from just the last few centuries whose work remains.

- And what shall we say of movies, television, and speechmaking? Even though only a few will make their names here, still these entertainments are fleeting and ephemeral, holding influence for a generation or two before fading.

Things that people find enduringly valuable are valuable because they speak across time.

- Paintings of the hunt drawn on a cave wall 25,000 years ago call to us today because they contain a fundamental truth: we are part of nature, and we must fight for our position in the world.

- The Venus of Willendorf fertility statute of a similar age carries a similar message: we want some part of us to continue, to survive the ages.

- What better way than passing our genes through our children and their children? Every person alive today can trace their ancestry back to a common parent if we unravel the tapestry of genealogy sufficiently far back.

Fiction in the form of plays and theater amuse us for an evening. Those that endure are the ones that elaborate on fundamental aspects of human nature.

- Tragedy, comedy, pride, these we can recognize immediately, though they are acted out on a stage thousands of years old.

- Shakespeare's renown is unmatched, not only or even chiefly because he wrote so well, but because he wrote with insight about our true passions and desires, of the human condition in all its folly, foibles, and majesty.

Philosophy is aimed at uncovering enduring truths. The human condition has changed little since the first civilizations emerged.

People were worried about living a good life thousands of years ago, and chances are good that they will be interested in this question a few thousand years from now.

What is human thought, what drives human motivation, and what guides human interaction? Address these questions, dear reader, and you will never lack an attentive audience.

History will enshroud almost all of us in murkiness as surely as death shrouds our worn-out bodies. Most or all of what we do will be lost. Make your efforts meaningful to the human condition and you may extend your renown beyond your lifetime if that is what you want.

Of the billions who have gone before us, precious few have made a lasting mark, and even fewer because of the office they briefly held. If you wish to represent more than a ripple from a pebble tossed in a pond, bend your efforts toward answering questions of basic human motivation.

And to do this, you need *less* of the company of your fellow man, not *more* of it. To think deeply and correctly, you need solitude. You need to make space for your thoughts to ramble, you need stillness for your voice to be heard.

We all know that one cannot serve two masters well. When you are about the affairs of the state, you cannot state the true nature of affairs to yourself, let alone others.

Rather than watching your pebbles vanish into the depths, carefully place your foundation on solid ground. Lay your stones one atop another, until the tower you have erected can be seen from the horizon and stand for the ages. This is surely difficult for all of us, and it is the reason that so few manage to make a lasting impression.

I will pay you today with a cornerstone, on which you may continue to build. For this stone may be used over and over, by builders of every kind. It comes from the workshop of Epictetus, whose chisels rang out with this truth:

> Wealth consists not in having great possessions,
> but in having few wants.

I have drilled this lesson into you to such an extent that I need not elaborate. Today I urge you to note that you may apply the principle of this proverb to many areas of human endeavor.

- Do you wish to accomplish great things? Do not attempt to do more but focus on less. Better pick a single priority and focus on it until you have found success than to spray your efforts like mist in a hurricane.

- Do you yearn for better relationships? Rather than numbering your Facebook friends in the hundreds, lavish your time and attention on your family.

- Are you looking for the perfect vacation or trip or experience? It is folly to cast your nets wildly in every direction in the hopes of catching a prize. Bait a single hook and sit quietly in one place until you have calmed your mind. You will realize that satisfaction cannot be fished up by dredging anywhere other than within you.

TLDR (too long; didn't read)? I leave you with a gift from the Greek tragedian Euripides, which encapsulates the lessons of this letter:

> Our lives ... are but a little while, so let them run as sweetly as you can, and give no thought to grief from day to day. For time is not concerned to keep our hopes, but hurries on its business, and is gone.

Euripides advises us to pay no heed to what bothers us daily, for fear the daily troubles become thieves of our happiness. His words survived for centuries because he spoke of human values, not because he was aiming for fame.

Be well.

Chapter Six

On Sticking to Your Decisions

Whether you are advancing or retreating, be fully committed to what you are doing

E ach person has to take their own stock of when is the proper time to step away from their working life. It will be different for different people, with different safety nets deemed necessary, and no one else can determine this for you.

I caution you though, dear reader, don't make yourself unhappy while you are pondering your future. Whether you are advancing or retreating, be fully committed to what you are doing.

Make it your business to do a good job with what is before you, and the next step comes more easily and naturally for you and all around you. If, rather, you make yourself miserable by musing on what you have not yet achieved, you are sabotaging your chances of success.

Accepting your tasks and doing your very best at what is before you also means embracing the consequences of your decisions.

Who cares what other people think about success, accomplishment, and living a good life? Others do not live with the consequences of your decisions, you do. If you are properly guided by your own thoughts, and achieve the outcomes you intended, what of it that another has set their sights differently?

I wrote to you about standing out among the many who will be forgotten. An iconoclast will stand out by challenging conventional wisdom. Do not challenge the status quo for the sake of being contrarian, but simply to ensure you come to your own conclusions, and that you think for yourself.

I consider Steve Jobs a modern-day skeptic; he put it this way:

> Your time is limited, don't waste it living someone else's life. Don't be trapped by dogma, which is living the result of other people's thinking. Don't let the noise of others' opinions drown out your own inner voice.

What would I tell those just embarking on their careers?

- I would tell them not to fear failure, but rather to make sure they learn from every experience. It is more harmful to your prospects not to try than it is to mess up every now and then.

- Next, consider that those who have gone before you thought just like you did. As a result, try to imagine *why* they did what they did before you try to tear it down.

- Finally, chase growth, not money, at least as soon as you have enough money to pay for your basic needs, and use development as your metric to decide when to make a change.

Once you have made up your mind to change your job or give it up altogether, the decision on how to proceed is entirely up to you. To successfully execute, you must reconcile yourself to a change in circumstance, that is all.

If you seek retirement, yes, you will relinquish the office, the company car, the perks, and some status. Decide what you love more: The trappings or your freedom.

And remember this, my dear reader, many complain without end about the burdens associated with their position. But if it is your position that affords you advantages you can't afford to live without, what sense is there in complaining? You are held captive by your desires, and so you desire your captivity.

There must be an end to desires. You can never earn enough if you measure your worth by your earnings.

But you can take none of your wealth or the possessions they enable you to buy with you into death. And many more do not survive their wealth, in the sense that the pursuit of wealth drives them to an early grave.

You can take nothing of your belongings with you. Consider the Pharaohs' elaborate tombs and burial chambers, filled to overflowing with material goods. Though their spirits passed away, their possessions stayed resolutely behind.

My finger hovered once more over the send button until I realized you are missing your customary words of wisdom.

To show you that lessons may be drawn from any source and that it is the content that counts and not the wrapper it comes in, I offer you inspiration from the American televangelist Robert Schuller:

> I'd rather attempt to do something great and fail
> than to attempt to do nothing and succeed.

View your decisions over the course of your career as a grand adventure. They deserve your best effort and undivided attention, and you shall be as dedicated as any general is to their campaign. Once you have made a decision, commit to it with the fervor of Cortés in his colonization of the Americas.

Though you do not burn your bridges, for you can always use connections to those who have journeyed with you and helped you along the way, by all means, burn your ship so that there may be no retreat from your chosen path.

Be well.

Chapter Seven

On Instagram-Worthy Quotes

You mustn't take the headline for the whole of the message but rather read on

What has become of my closing quotes, you wonder, where I shared wisdom collected from sages across the ages. Am I no longer able to reinforce each letter with the lessons duly noted from earlier masters?

Fear not, my store of pithy sayings has not been depleted.

The Stoics alone numbered many who became adept at condensing their knowledge into rich kernels, making them easy to pass on and share. One sees their influence across the intervening centuries, in students as diverse as Shakespeare, C.S. Lewis, and Steve Jobs.

The Stoics, in turn, represent but a fraction of notable thinkers who have grappled with great truths. Thus, from sources without end, we have a rich menu of maxims to choose from.

Moreover, for any single idea, you can call upon ten or twenty formulations, each of which either reiterates or reformulates a central theme.

The sayings we collect and repeat do serve laudable purposes: They whet our appetites to know more, they refresh our memory of what we have already studied, and they provide a glimpse through an opened window of what truths lie beyond.

But just as the container is not the content, the maxim is not the full message, only a key for interpreting the map. Though one may memorize a thousand sayings, and repeat them back in any setting, are they any better than a trained parrot?

A chatbot may respond to any of a hundred programmed questions, but are you having a meaningful interaction? Alexa on your countertop has become your daily conversationalist, but if you probe beneath the surface will you find anything of substance?

Thus I caution you, my dear reader, that to know why an idea is worthy of study at all, you need to digest more than Instagram-worthy morsels. Such light fare may be eagerly sought by the masses, but not the sincere student.

You mustn't take the headline for the whole of the message but rather read on. Read widely and deeply.

I want you to walk the grounds that gave root to an idea, wallow in the soil that nourished it, and be drenched by the summer storms that gave it strength. If you tend to the garden of ideas in this way, you will know not only how the fruits there came to ripen, but you will enjoy an abundant harvest.

Now consider this: No matter how strong the seed stock you start with, would you be a mere tender of another's crop, or will you add something new to the storehouse of humankind's bounty?

When you are the master of your garden, you can cross-pollinate ideas and bring whole new lineages of thought into being.

I think that although you may start out with what others thought, you need to end up with what you think.

Be well.

Chapter Eight

On a Successor's Success

If the sincere student is not ready, the teacher is not done

I cannot tell you what joy it brings me to be well replaced! To know that what you have built will be maintained and expanded is to know that you have not toiled in vain.

The master carpenter lays down tools all the more willingly when the apprentice is waiting and eager to take them up.

How to explain, then, the many who clutch jealously to the reins and refuse to relinquish them?

We talked elsewhere about the dangers of mistaking one's work for one's meaning. Besides those who have not found their purpose outside their labor, I suspect what keeps many in the saddle well beyond their comfort is fear.

This fear comes in two forms: First, that their successor will outshine them, and second, that they will not.

"What can this mean?" you ask. "How can both the one and its opposite be the culprit?"

They are alike, my dear reader, in that they both arise from flawed thinking about the relationship between teacher and student.

- The one who is afraid of being outdone does not understand that the renown of the student reflects favorably on their teacher.

- And while the other avoids this particular trap, they have fallen prey to another: Namely, lacking confidence that they have done enough to prepare their pupil.

- Just as renown redounds to the teacher, so too does failure lie properly at their feet. For if the master fears the student is not ready, does the apt pupil not also know it?

It is folly to hand over the keys while sweating and flinching at the thought of what the new driver will do on their first solo trip.

If the sincere student does not understand, the teacher has not been clear. If the sincere student is not ready, the teacher is not done.

Humankind progresses when we do our utmost to ensure that the steps we've taken do not need to be retraced and that the lessons we've learned are not lost.

Consider how much farther the next runner in the relay race can advance if we take care that they do not start behind us, but rather from the very tip of the baton in our outstretched hand.

Just as you are a sincere student, I aim to be no false teacher. I rejoice in seeing you progress, as much for my own sake as your own, because it means I am fulfilling my duty as you fulfill your promise.

Be well.

Chapter Nine

On Defining Your Own Success

To follow your own mind, especially when it directs a course that goes against all others, is the greatest achievement

If you would be a true friend to your friend, then advise him to stand firm on his decision to stand down from his position. The title, the prestige, the pay, these are but little compared to his peace of mind.

The many who challenge him and call him crazy for quitting in his prime do not know him. If you consider how hard we must work to know ourselves, what chance is there that another knows us better?

No, the critics flail about not because they know his heart, but for another reason: To go along with the crowd is comforting because it requires no thought.

When one pushes off confidently in another direction, they must be crazy, for otherwise what does it say about the crowd? People will happily convict a person who challenges their unspoken convictions so as to avoid challenging themselves to think.

"He is lazy," claims this one. "He is afraid of failure," says the next.

When people accuse others, they often are giving you a window into themselves. Because our imagination is weak, we see in others the things we feel in ourselves.

And I do not need to tell you that there is another kind of friend, the one who wishes secretly to see you fail. Your value to such a friend is that they feel superior to you.

This one does not rejoice in your joy but feels only envy when seeing your success.

Upon seeing one who, knowing his own mind and dealing honestly with the results of his thoughts, makes a hard decision, do we give courage or cast doubt?

You are no false friend. As such, congratulate your friend that he has finally come to know himself.

To do what everyone does requires no thought and little effort. To follow your own mind, especially when it directs a course that goes against all others, is the greatest achievement.

Compared to this, no amount of riches or power amounts to anything. And without self-possession, no amount of possessions will satisfy.

If you wish to capture success, the greatest weapon you can arm yourself with is not a physical thing.

- It is not bargained for with money, or even bought with bonds of loyalty.

- Though you surround yourself with things to serve as legions of defenders on every front, still the enemy slinks undetected into your tent and into your thoughts.

To protect yourself from harm, you do not need to add to your army but rather subtract from it: lose the fear of loss and give up wants.

If you yourself can take these things away, no one can take anything from you. Then you will have cleared the field and made the way for satisfaction and joy to win the day.

Be well.

Chapter Ten

On Bosses and Underlings

It betrays real cruelty to knowingly treat another as beneath you simply because they serve you

I am pleased to observe that you behave the same no matter the company you are with. You can tell much about a person by how they treat those around them.

"That's just an employee," your colleagues will say. Are we not all employed in one pursuit or another?

"Servant!" Yes, and do you not also serve many masters?

"Stranger!" No, they are but one we haven't met yet.

Reflect how often we would treat worse those whom we know nothing about, who have done us no harm, over those we know best and who have surely given us cause for complaint.

I wrote you that your social class is no bar to becoming a philosopher. Why then does achieving an elevated status serve for so many as a barrier to treating people well?

We all know the executive who scurries from the door of their chauffeured limousine to the express elevator waiting to whisk them to the top floor of their building.

- A selection of powerful seconds-in-command is on hand to fill their ears with affirmations before they adjourn to the executive dining room to fill their bellies with delicacies.

- And should they need relief after their indulgence, they retire to their private bathrooms where they discreetly conduct another sort of business.

They imagine their power makes them lonely because no one can understand the burdens they bear. Undisturbed in their isolation, they think they are unobserved.

Better see them for what they are, which is unobservant, for a horde of underlings circles around them always:

- Who chauffeured them from their manor to the office, or kept the lobby clear of obstacles and the elevator doors open and waiting?

- Who keeps the printer toned and full of paper, the trashcans emptied, and gilded faucets gleaming?

- Does the food so tastefully described in the menu of the day materialize unaided by human hands, like the miracle of the loaves and fishes?

I suspect the boss who fears having too frequent interaction with the common employee knows the encounter risks reminding both that their differences are slight.

Better that they surround themselves with the trappings of power, reinforcing a distinction in appearance if not in substance. Though if they only paused to consider what sort of difference they were drawing with this thinking, they might think twice.

Give one person a low position and raise another up high. Have you done anything to either's sharp hearing, far-seeing, or clear thinking?

The lowly perceive in an instant every false note from their bosses, just as those seniors are shutting their senses to all beneath them.

Worse than the boss who blinds themselves to what is going on around them is the boss who convinces themselves that they have become better by virtue of their elevation.

They may have failed basic math and be hopeless at adding single-digit sums without a calculator, but they become geniuses at calculating their respective status on the social ladder.

There is no sadder spectacle than a boss who berates their secretary while toadying up to the board committee members overseeing compensation.

It betrays real cruelty to knowingly treat another as beneath you simply because they serve you. But to do so out of ignorance of their inherent worth is an even worse offense to your own worth.

For what kind of person says a colleague is to be prized because of their tailored suit and Rolex watch, while another is base because they lack them?

I will tell you what kind of person, dear reader, and pray you do not find yourself among their number.

You have seen this person out of their business setting but still in their element: they stroll without a blush to the front of the security line because they are in a hurry and have a plane to catch.

It effortlessly escapes their attention that every person they've walked past has an identical objective, and some will be on the same plane, and it is as well they have averted their gaze for they would otherwise see murder in a thousand eyes.

Well before you arrive at the restaurant door, you hear this person enunciate the words that serve as their passport to prominence, "Don't you know who I am!"

It is a declarative statement, not a question, for no answer other than an abject apology for the delay is acceptable. What goes unsaid by the maître' d' and all others in earshot is this: "I know exactly who you are, and you are a fool."

But this person is a fool who will be gladly suffered for the sake of parting them with their folding cash.

When you are welcomed with air kisses and open arms into the boutique or gallery that would turn away all but the most well-heeled, consider whether it is your person or your wallet that is being courted.

Things that have true value are not counted in money. People are not properly measured by their outward appearance.

A boss that places their faith in money and appearances may gain both in the short term, but it is their fate to be forgotten.

They retire to their golf courses on the East Coast barrier islands, and no one marks their passing as a loss. Though their gated communities are virtual barriers to the poor, they are nonetheless filled with the unworthy.

Be well.

Chapter Eleven

On Dangerous Goals

How many unhappy professionals do we know who, upon reaching the pinnacle of supposed success, are plagued by doubts about whether the sacrifices were worth the prize?

You thought your parents, teachers, and friends wanted what's best for you.

From your earliest days, they told you "You can do anything you want. You can be anyone you want!" Though our cheerleaders may wish us well, in practice their statements have the worst of effects on us.

Even when every hand would lift us up, still we are weighed down by others' expectations when we make them our own. Better that we were nurtured by wolves than have our expectations raised to such heights.

The YouTuber who becomes a millionaire in their teens. The rapper who becomes a star in their twenties, flashing brilliance along with their golden chains and diamond watches.

For every astronaut, celebrity baker, senator, or hedge fund billionaire, there are countless watchers who set their goals accordingly: I will be rich, I will be powerful, I will be famous.

When you set any of these as your goal, you set yourself on a path of guaranteed hardship and likely disappointment.

It is a lucky few who learn at the end what they should have asked themselves at the beginning: How can I be happy?

There are two problems with goals, dear reader: The first is that in themselves goals do not contain the blueprint for success only the seeds of suffering.

They are a marker for what you say you want, but they give no clue as to the roads you must choose and how steep will be the tolls you pay to travel towards your destination.

The second problem is that goals guarantee dissatisfaction unless and until they have been reached, by which time the damage wrought in their seeking often outweighs the benefit you hoped for.

How many unhappy professionals do we know who, upon reaching the pinnacle of supposed success, are plagued by doubts about whether the sacrifices were worth the prize?

How many celebrities who decry the relentless intrusion of the very attention they so desperately sought to attract?

Conspicuous consumption is noticeably absent from the habits of the wise person with a well-ordered mind.

If by wanting things you find yourself wanting for peace and satisfaction, leave off the setting of such goals and set yourself to understanding the value of things.

You can never achieve that which you do not understand, even though the ingredients for your success may be stored away in your pantry to pick up at will.

You cannot satisfy your hunger until you understand it is a sickness of the mind that ails you and not a lack of nourishment.

Cure your illness by cutting off the source of the pathogen that infects you: the expectations of others, and your own ill-considered goals.

Be well.

Chapter Twelve

On Private and Public Service

The true meaning of public service is not those offices that are most visible, but those deeds that have the greatest impact

We do things in the reverse order: We encourage young people into public service and positions of power before they have learned wisdom, and we urge our elders to withdraw from public view when they are most likely to be of service to humankind.

At different stages of their lives, each person should consider how they can make a contribution to the world, and this starts with learning how to better themselves.

A broken ruler will never yield a straight line, no matter how many times you put it to service, so your first task is to learn what is true.

Rarely does an education in life come for free, though you may not pay the tuition in money. Experience is a hard teacher, dear reader. I would have said unforgiving, but that's not true. For though we cannot control everything that comes our way, the consequences are applied evenly for all.

The teacher of life is strict but consequent, and a lesson learned need not be repeated. The fact that some of our companions may need multiple sessions is not the fault of the professor but of the inattentive student.

A sincere student is watchful, attentive, and above all humble. To know when you do not know is to gain the key that will open the door to wisdom.

Certainty is a key that will turn many locks but open no doors.

Think of your life as a series of stages. In your youth and early adult years, you should be best friends with curiosity. Be a sleuth, observe much, say little. Inquisitiveness is your watchword.

Strive to make every sentence begin with "Why …?" Most of what you hear in response will be wrong, misguided, or irrelevant. Scattered among the inaccuracies will be grains of truth, but how to tell which is which?

You will note that what people say and what they do are rarely in harmony. Listen to their words and watch carefully their deeds. Gaining an insight into the human motivations behind both talking and doing gives you X-ray-like perception, allowing you to see beneath the surface of things.

In time, you will develop rough models for not just how the world works, but also why. Incentives are everything and I will come back to this another time.

In the second stage, let's call it middle age though it may come at any age, you will have working hypotheses. You will be able to say the words, "In my experience ..." and it will not be the start of an empty sentence.

You will still watch more than you talk, because you are conducting experiments to test your hypotheses, not yet publishing the conclusions of your studies.

Besides checking whether your predictions regarding people and events are accurate, you may begin to wonder how best to direct the course of events.

If what people say is an unfaithful guide to their actions, and they can be influenced without even realizing their minds are not their own, may you not put human motivation to use for your own purposes?

By this time in your life, most of your peers will have given up on trying to see behind the complexity of affairs and will accept the surface appearance of things. They will not think explicitly this is so, but their convictions about how the world works will steadily calcify, reinforced by the fact that everyone else believes the same as they do.

When all around you say, "More money is good, more responsibility is best, more possessions are pleasurable," who are they to disagree?

This is when you are at your most dangerous and when you must watch yourself with the vigilance of a prison guard whose every inmate has escaped multiple times before. For you are like a child grasping a sharp knife. You know that it cuts deeply, and which end is pointed, but you do not wield it confidently or accurately.

At the next stage, your values become paramount because they are put to the test. For the first time, you have the power to direct the course of events in a material way. The young student may not know much, but they also cannot influence much.

You have learned much, including not only how and why things work, but also how to make them go in the direction of your choosing. Will you be wise in your choices?

For with your greater insight, you are now in a position to make choices on behalf of others, not just yourself. Though the sheep believe they are making their own choices within the comfort of the herd, the shepherd knows they are controlling the flock's direction, guiding and steering with a tap here, a word there, a sharp whistle from time to time.

In this third stage of your life, you are ready to make the move away from the private service of bettering yourself towards the public service of bettering humankind.

This does not mean you must take up public office. That is but one possible avenue of service, fraught with many pitfalls and as much likelihood of doing harm as doing good.

For most, I say you are better served by serving in obscurity. Best that none know your name or position, though your influence may be widely felt.

"Why is this?" you ask, "What is the harm in being transparent and gaining recognition for your works?"

The risk in prominence is two-fold, dear reader. The first comes from yourself, and the second comes from others. To the first risk, when you act for the benefit of others, fame and recognition are false currency, feeding your pride more than they do your reason.

The reward for being altruistic cannot be to burnish your vanity. Otherwise, your own motivations will be corrupted to gain acclaim rather than to do good. Only infrequently will you find these two in harmonious company. You must maintain a watchful guard over your mind to stay alert, for your wisdom has not permanently vanquished your ego, only temporarily subdued it.

The egos of the masses present then your second risk. Do you think any will be happy to learn of your manipulations? That you have had not only the idea but also practice trying to influence their actions?

That you say it is for their own good will not dim their outrage. Do you think they will delight in hearing that everything they value, all they have placed stock in, has been misguided?

We would rather be told sweet lies, blindfolded and only steps away from the guillotine, than be told that we are naked and exposed with a long way to go till paradise.

Tell the truth at your peril, for the ignorant will not understand, the wicked will not care, and the great many will hate you for making them doubt their own beliefs.

Thus, you must serve in silence if you wish to preserve your ability to maneuver. The greatest good is done by those with the least need to talk about it. The true meaning of public service is not those offices that are most visible, but those deeds that have the greatest impact.

And remember this: You may change the world more with a single honest idea than you do by leading the mightiest army.

Be well.

Chapter Thirteen

On Business as a Distraction

It is impatience in business affairs, as much as in life, that leads us to be distracted from potentially more valuable pursuits

There is a feeling I've had more than once lately, dear reader, and it is an unwelcome one even though I know I bring it fully upon myself.

You ask me a question and I recognize the topic. I am familiar with the issue, and I know I have worked on it at length before. But I do not recall enough of the answer to feel confident that I should speak without refreshing my memory.

Once not long past I had all my thoughts firmly about my person, available for ready use at a moment's notice, "without a thought," so to speak. Now I fear that I am shedding recollections like cats and dogs shed their hair: Carelessly, profligately.

I have scattered behind me a steady trail of thoughts in WIKI entries, chats, emails, memos, and one-pagers. Like Hansel and Gretel thinking their breadcrumbs would remain untouched such that they could retrace their steps, I am probably wrong to assume I will be able to call indefinitely upon my own markers to recall my state of mind when I created them.

Thus, I will not answer your latest question off the top of my head. I need consultation with my crumbs before I can reply to you, my dear reader. I trust you are not so impatient as to require an immediate response, in which case I would have to rely on my gut rather than my head.

It is impatience in business affairs, as much as in life, that leads us to be distracted from potentially more valuable pursuits. There is always something urgent clamoring for our attention and often enough we are confronted with a perceived or actual crisis that crowds out everything else.

When our hair is on fire, it seems only natural to postpone all that is not urgent and tend to the flames, but this runs the risk of forever keeping us from attending to that which is important.

To be the director of your own play, to stage your own actions rather than being danced about like a marionette on invisible strings, this seems like the greatest luxury to the busy worker. It is a kind of torture to feel pulled by events toward actions you would otherwise not have chosen to pursue.

All the more so when you are aware of the time lost from your studies in pursuit of a well-ordered mind. I think this is why so many give up trying to control the turbulent flow of work that streams into their office. To fight against the current is a herculean task, and not one that many can maintain for long.

"I already know what you're going to say," I can hear you sigh. But do not despair, dear reader, for my message today is not one of hardship and sacrifice, or at least not toil without end.

Yes, it is true I do not counsel you to "go with the flow," because this carries you only to places you do not wish to go. But nor will I urge you to swim upstream. Rather, turn your gaze to either shore of the river, and start to make your way to dry ground.

Though you are still being carried along by the raging waters, you can swim the short distance to the shore. What awaits you on the banks? Nothing more than the realization that though you do not recall diving or being pushed into the water, no one and nothing forces you to stay in and drown.

You can be content by not competing for the same carnival prizes that all your companions scramble after. Your happiness need not be related to your busyness, or your success in business. Your possessions need number little more than your self-possession.

If your mind is the motor that propels you along in life, your reason is the rudder that helps you steer around obstacles and put safely into port. Would you scrape off barnacles, scrub the decks spotless, and maintain everything on your boat except the motor? Would you be eager to board a charter when you observed no one's hand was on the rudder?

Why then do you think you'll be well served in responding to every urgency of business when this prevents you from the all-important business of maintaining your mind?

Rather than praying for a drought to dry up the stream of your desires, take seriously the duties of captain and carefully steer your ship away from useless wants and groundless fears. The

Coast Guard is not coming to save you, you must save yourself by setting yourself free.

If you will allow me to stretch the analogy a bit more: You save yourself by donning the life vest of philosophy, grasping tight to the lessons we have been discussing lest you lose the progress you have made.

If you feel at this moment like you would rather slip under the waters if only it meant you would not need to hear me urging you on, then use the words of Naval Ravikant instead of my own as the lighthouse to guide your way:

> I value freedom above everything else. All kinds of freedom: freedom to do what I want, freedom from things I don't want to do, freedom from my own emotions or things that may disturb my peace.

I value you too much, dear reader, to let you go unaided. I will continue to offer my assistance for so long as I am able.

Be well.

Chapter Fourteen

On Losing One's Mind

Am I of sound mind when I tell you I believe I can control the elements? You need but lace up your shoes and join me to experience the phenomenon yourself

Y ou asked me to relay the details of my day and to omit nothing. This must mean you have developed a tolerance for my overly wrought descriptions.

Perhaps you feel my actions will serve as an example of how to behave yourself, in which case you are placing great faith in me as your teacher. Or could it be that you have digested well the lesson of mine that a person serves as an example regardless of the merit of their behavior: If they behave wisely you may emulate them, but if they are foolish tell yourself to avoid their mistakes.

Either way, let my day be your object lesson today!

The course of my days has changed in recent times as I have moved from being master over others to focusing more on being master over myself.

For years I woke to the blare of an alarm clock, pulled usually from some fitful dream brought on by obsessive attention to a topic. A difficult employee situation, a contract dispute, an intense strategy session.

Other times it was a recurring travel nightmare my alarm freed me from. No matter how many times I travel, and I once traveled every week in four crisscrossing the globe, I dream I will be late — to wake, to catch the train, to check-in, to board the plane, to make the connection, and so on in a series of endless ways to lose out by losing time.

However drawn from slumber, my routine was to dress and have a quick bowl of cereal while catching up on emails before getting in my car and driving the half hour to the office.

This commute was the quietest time of my day and I used it to change my mental state: On the way to work to get in the necessary hardened mindset and on the way home to leave that hardness behind and become fit for family interaction.

At work, twelve hours would pass, and I will spare you a recitation of those details so as not to unnecessarily strain your politeness. Suffice it to say that I learned to tell myself regularly that upholding the rule of law is so vital to a healthy society that it must justify even the most mundane lawyerly tasks.

And though I needed to thus fortify my tasks in my head to consider them vital, still the days would often pass without my noticing the time. It was only upon looking up and seeing the sun was long gone that I realized my kids would already be asleep in their beds and my dinner tucked away under plastic wrap, and take once more to the now empty roads on my solitary commute home.

But you were not asking what I *used* to do, patient reader, but what I *do now*. I ask you to indulge this reminiscence if only to draw a contrast to a typical day today.

You know I have reduced my work pensum to 50%, though compared to the hours I formerly toiled, in actuality I have gained back far more than half my day. I have largely laid claim for myself the first half of each day and have been experimenting with different pursuits in this newly found freedom.

I wake now to the rhythm of nature and my body. I have let the battery in my alarm clock dim and die as I often wished it would when I was working. If I need time to sleep and to dream, I take it.

When I awaken, I indulge in a cup of coffee before I leave the snug ensconce of my bed. This simple pleasure brings me such satisfaction. Aaahhh. Caffeine is a vice I will gladly continue to suffer if such benefits can be had at such a small price.

I first started by reading the newspaper in bed, cover to cover while still safely under my covers. This too was an indulgence, for I never had time to linger on any story before. No more would I skim the headlines for anything relevant to our business, perhaps some regulatory development or an enforcement action we should be concerned about.

Though it seemed a small luxury to read at my leisure, I began to feel this came at the much greater cost of my peace of mind. This is a threat to my reason that I cannot afford to let linger.

I don't know when it happened exactly, dear reader, but the news has turned from the business of informing minds to the business of inflaming passions. When profits are driven by clicks, and outrage keeps readers engaged, should we be surprised when our reporters turn to fiction? What they do not invent, they cherry-pick to present the most extreme side of every story.

Habits are truly our friend, though, in helping to both cultivate the good and excise the bad. By simply not picking up my iPad, I soon did not miss reading the paper in the morning or indeed at all. The few times I was drawn in again come evening, I was amazed at how irrelevant the day's news felt as the day drew to a close.

I do of course eventually arise from my bed, lest you think I spend not just the night on my back but also the day. Now up, my self-directed pursuits are found in reading, writing, and running, often in that order.

Instead of descending into shameful reporting that leaves me feeling tainted for having read it, I may pick up a letter from Seneca to Lucilius to see what these old friends were discussing and to what end. This usually inspires me to write to you and see if I can wrestle some thoughts from my head onto the page.

And when I feel the need for a break from mental gymnastics, I switch from exercising my mind to exercising my legs.

Though I run alone most days, I feel like I have a multitude with me. There are first the voices of the scholars I have been reading and communing with. I hear them as if they were talking aloud. I argue with them, imagining they are running beside me to hear my words.

I try to have five or six companions such as this at any given time. Right now they include Seneca, Epictetus, Confucius, Richard Feynman, and Jordan Peterson.

Later in the summer as the days lengthen and warm, I plan to have Cicero, Marcus Aurelius, and Charlie Munger joining me. I also want to visit once more with my former running partners, Jean Jacques Rousseau, John Stuart Mill, John Rawls, and the Federalist Papers.

In fact, I feel the Olympic stadium is filled with onlookers who at a moment's notice can be beckoned down from the stands to rejoin the race. We are blessed to have so many companions to choose from.

I cherish these voices, as much as I do yours, my dear reader, because they help drown out my own insistent thoughts. This is the one voice I can never outrun.

You would think after more than 20 years of running I would have learned to accept my limits, to know what I can safely do, and what I should leave to younger, fitter men.

But how easily I can bring to mind my old running coach, Martin. He is the kindest of persons though he has a mad glint peeking out behind his easy smile. That glint says "Go ahead, I dare you! Let's see how much you can do. Run as fast as you like, I'll never be further than one step behind you."

Truly we ran in fear of his imagined pitchfork at our backs as much as we did for the joy of it. I now carry with me in my brain my own mad Martin, urging me on and saying crazy things. It is best to pay that voice little heed, except perhaps when I need him to finish a race.

So, I find solace in these other companions, though I do all the work of carrying them with me on my rounds.

My madness does not stop with these thoughts about running. I would go so far as to tell you that I am reliably insane in several other areas.

For one, I am as gullible as Charlie Brown when Lucy invites him yet again to kick the football from her treacherous hands. My downfall is the weather app on my phone. How many times have I been fooled by a forecast only to find myself cursing the weather gods in the middle of a downpour?

Refusing to learn at least this lesson is apparently also habit-forming, for no matter how many times I find myself flung into a momentary rage upon needing to wring myself dry, still I check the forecast every single time before I set foot outside the door.

I would do better consulting the Farmer's Almanack from last century for tomorrow's weather. At least then I would have no illusions about what to expect.

Am I of sound mind when I tell you I believe I can control the elements, dear reader? You need but lace up your shoes and join me to experience the phenomenon yourself.

- When we start out on the path together you will marvel at the bracing headwind that whisks away our sweat.

- Though we run an out-and-back course, or even run in circles, you will marvel even more to note that the headwind prevails no matter our direction.

- Or consider the course that you would swear was flat when we ran it one way, but which turns into a hill upon our return.

- Just today I experienced a horizontal wall of rain (unforecasted of course) driven by a wind so strong that sailors' spouses would quail in fear that their loved ones would safely come home.

As god of the elements, I just hold onto my hat and keep putting one foot in front of the other.

My insanity is at least temporary, for I do not give it a long leash outside the arena of running. Pity those who lose control of their minds on a more permanent basis.

I am talking about the afflictions of envy, anger, and greed. Many give themselves over fully to these passions, though it deprives them of their right reason and well-ordered mind.

I condemn too lust, if not love. We say a person is "head over heels" in love. If we consider what state of mind and what activities give rise to this condition, shouldn't we rather say the person is "heels over head" in lust?

Take care that you limit your own insanities to times and places where you can be sure of quickly regaining your mind. I do not ask you to be perfect at all times, but to be perfectly aware when you are not.

Be well.

www.ingramcontent.com/pod-product-compliance
Lightning Source LLC
Chambersburg PA
CBHW060428050426
42449CB00009B/2195